Ideas Are Your
Only Currency

Rod Judkins is an accomplished lecturer at Central St Martin's, one of the world's pre-eminent art schools whose alumni - ranging from artists like Lucien Freud, and Antony Gormley through to the designers Stella McCartney and Alexander McQueen - have helped shape our culture. Judkins has lectured on the subject of creativity at universities and to businesses around the world. He blogs at *Psychology Today*, and also acts as a consultant to numerous private companies. Trained at The Royal College of Art, he has exhibited at galleries including Tate Britain, The National Portrait Gallery and The Royal Academy.

www.rodjudkins.com

Ideas Are Your Only Currency

Rod Judkins

SCEPTRE

First published in Great Britain in 2017 by Sceptre

An imprint of Hodder & Stoughton
An Hachette UK company

1

A CIP catalogue record for this title is available from the British Library

Hardback ISBN 978 1 473 64004 7
eBook ISBN 978 1 473 64006 1

Typeset by Craig Burgess
Printed and bound by Clays Ltd, St Ives plc

Hodder & Stoughton policy is to use papers that are natural,
renewable and recyclable products and made from wood grown in
sustainable forests. The logging and manufacturing processes
are expected to conform to the environmental regulations of the
country of origin.

Hodder & Stoughton Ltd
Carmelite House
50 Victoria Embankment
London EC4Y 0DZ

www.sceptrebooks.co.uk

This book is dedicated to Zelda, Scarlet and Louis

Introduction
ARE YOU DEAD?

'What skills and abilities will I need to prosper in five, ten, twenty years' time?'

This was the question I imagined myself being asked when I devised a course called '100 Design Projects' at Central Saint Martins, one of the world's pre-eminent art schools. I wanted to know how a generation could future-proof itself.

We all need to be prepared for a world that is fluid, global and interdisciplinary. Distinctions between specialties will blur and overlap. In this vortex there are no maps. Change used to happen over two or three generations. It took the West centuries to absorb the effects of Gutenberg's mechanical printing press. Now, change is instant. Computers, the Internet and other forms of technology reorder the world with alarming frequency. Innovative and creative thinkers, those who create products and services, now drive economies.

To prosper in economies of the future, then, you need to realise that the real currency of our age isn't money. It isn't data, attention or time.

It's ideas.

You're surrounded by ideas. Films, books, music, buildings, fashion, businesses of every size and scale – everything in your culture began life as a vision in someone's head. Ideas can trigger revolutions or nudge society in a particular direction, and they can spring from the unlikeliest people in bedrooms, garages, offices, classrooms or cafés. In the industrial era, you learnt a skill and were set up for life. In our post-industrial era, a skill becomes redundant as it's being learnt. You no longer need to be skilled, brilliant or talented to be at the heart of things, to guide not just your own life but the future of the world around you. You need to be an ideas person: adaptable, open minded, adept at problem-solving, a communicator, inventor, artist and entertainer.

The purpose of this book is to help you take a leap towards becoming that person. An Olympic athlete trains their body. A creative person has to exercise as hard, but train their imagination. Like an athlete jogging, lifting weights and stretching, the exercises in these pages will make your mind fit and lean enough to be an ideas generator, to develop your conceptual ability and creative potential – regardless of your background or profession. They are designed to encourage you to think beyond what is accepted and conventional.

I've put creative thinking into practice in many organisations. Due to the success of my book *The Art of Creative Thinking*, which has been published in a dozen languages around the world, I've been lucky enough to be invited to teach creative thinking workshops in science, medical, economic and business departments at universities. I've also spoken at banks, hospitals, airlines, pharmaceutical companies and many others because these organisations have realized creative thinking can help them solve seemingly intractable problems. I've delivered workshops at Samsung and Apple, and to chemists and physicists at the University of Namur in Belgium. At the Royal Free Hospital in London I demonstrated how applied medical science students could benefit from my techniques. They've realized creative thinking can help them solve problems conventional processes cannot. It's been eye-opening for me to see creativity put into practice by scientists and engineers. It is a key that unlocks doors scientific methods couldn't previously open.

Some of the projects may seem fanciful but they are all based on real tasks I've set the many diverse groups I've worked with. One exercise involves designing a virus. Why? I set this project to a group of fifty applied medical students at the Royal Free Hospital in London. If you want to understand something, it's important to observe and research it. But to deeply comprehend something, you have to design it from scratch. The students considered how their virus could most effectively infect the human body, reproduce, defend itself against the body's immune system and much more. They got into the mind of the virus. They saw infection from the virus's perspective. They gained a deeper understanding than if they'd simply attended lectures about viruses. During the time I spent at the Royal Free I realised the staff and students were already creative people producing original ideas. There is now a fruitful crossover between science and art. Designers interested in genetics and geneticists designing life.

An ideas person is never content; they always want to push in a new direction. They create new opportunities by asking intelligent, provocative and innovative questions. They are restlessly ambitious about creating better clothes, cars, planes, hospitals and worlds for everyone.

How do you find your way and do something worthwhile? Flooded with information from posters, advertising and television, most people tune out and become passive consumers. They read a blog, shop in a supermarket, watch TV, buy clothes, see a film, and download music. Like sponges they unquestioningly absorb ideas fed to them by schools, parents and friends. They are a sieve and culture washes through them. Ideas people cup their hands, collect the culture and kneed it into something worthwhile. As I wander around the studios at Central Saint Martins in the evenings and look at students' work from courses such as architecture, fashion and product design, many extraordinary things are happening. The architecture students are designing the buildings you'll live and work in, product designers produce the cars you'll drive, others are making the films you'll see, and the furniture you'll use. In short, they're imagining your future. Wouldn't you rather imagine it for yourself?

The contradictory phrase, 'Intelligent Optimist' is frequently used at Central Saint Martins to describe the creative. The intelligent are realists. They see things for what they are. They try not to let emotion cloud their judgment. On the other hand, optimists are delusional. They leap around like spring lambs, exploring for the sake of exploring. With playful eagerness they try to make the impossible possible. In a world of seemingly intractable social problems, how could someone clever be optimistic? The creative are a mixture of intelligence and optimism. They believe they can create better futures, but back it up with intellectual rigor. With a mixture of humor, realism and imagination they look for ways to improve our culture. Instead of mindlessly consuming, they mindfully create. This is the reason Central Saint Martins – where I've worked for one or two days a week for the last fifteen years – is the most internationally renowned college in the world. It has produced students such as fashion designers Alexander McQueen, John Galliano, Stella McCartney, artists Lucien Freud, Anthony Gormley, Gilbert and George, performers Pierce Brosnan and Joe Strummer of the Clash and composer Lionel Bart. All were at the cutting edge of their fields.

This book is a distillation of all the teaching methods I have seen practiced at CSM. You are being treated to the best projects I have taught over a period of years. The exercises in this book will help you to be an intelligent optimist, to open your eyes, see clearly and switch on your imagination.

The task of inventing the future could take any form, therefore this book sees design as having no restrictions. The projects range across all disciplines: advertising, packaging, illustration, architecture, typography, furniture design, genetic engineering and many others. They are suitable for people from any background or any age, from a three-year-old to a ninety-nine-year-old. There are ten themes, each explore an important aspect of contemporary culture such as technology, time, the body, power and the future. There are ten exercises in each theme and they all push at the boundaries of design with the intention of developing your conceptual thinking.

Students who have produced the most successful results for these exercises don't search for the 'right' answer but look for the most unusual, surprising or amusing result. They generate many alternatives, then pick the most effective. Quite often absurd ideas lead to unexpected and powerful results. You don't have to be technically good at design or drawing; getting the idea across is what's important and a few scribbled lines can communicate an idea successfully. Aim to seek innovative and surprising solutions and avoid the predictable or formulaic. Make mistakes. Keep a flexible mind and consider all possibilities, the mass-produced or hand made, ornamental or functional, humble or monumental and high or low tech.

Ultimately, all conceptual design thinking is about the search for meaning. How can we communicate more effectively? What is the essence of this object? How does it shape our perceptions? Is there a limit to what we can we communicate? How can we create better cities? Ideas are important because what we think about the world and ourselves determines what we will become. This book challenges you to explore modern culture and therefore, yourself.

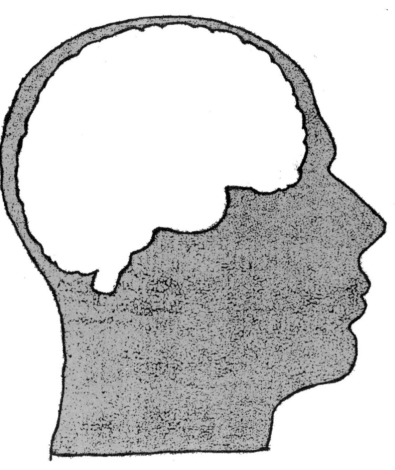

BEFORE GOING ANY FURTHER,
DRAW THE CONTENTS OF
YOUR MIND. YOU'LL BE ASKED
TO DO THIS AGAIN LATER.

Are you the tool of your tools?

Do you control technology or does it control you? We make technology and then it makes us. The flint axe, the printing press and the computer transformed our thinking. They're ubiquitous, so we use them thoughtlessly. You need to be aware of how they affect your thinking so you can use them and not be used by them.

'The medium is the message,' declared Marshall McLuhan, the great American philosopher of communication theory, in the mid-1960s. What he meant was that all media are an extension of the human senses. They expand our ability to interact with the world and alter our experience of it. The messages you or I send on social media seem important to us but what really matters is the way social media has changed our perceptions. The mechanism that drives it is sharing. This informs and empowers previously ignored communities.

Technology has widespread communal and philosophical consequences. McLuhan predicted a Global Village where technology brought humanity back to the interconnectedness of the tribal mentality. But we are more connected than he imagined. On our devices we can view emails, photos, work, videos, music and our whole life wherever we are. We get nervous if we're away from our computers or our cell phones for long. When on holiday, we're not on holiday. We're simply at work sitting by the pool. We're never off limits.

How do we take back control? We must upgrade our thinking and tune in to new mediums so that we can use them more effectively, and master them before they master us.

Once a new technology rolls over you, if you're not part of the steamroller, you're part of the road.

Stewart Brand

Are we devolving?

Scientists believe we are. Originally only the fittest survived to pass on their traits. But modern man didn't need to be physically strong to survive. Reliance on technology has caused our evolutionary downfall. Limbs get feebler due to inactivity, immune systems weaken as we rely on antibiotics and we're filling up with pacemakers, artificial joints and implants. Predict the future! Show us how man will devolve.

If it was possible to evolve, it was also possible to devolve, and that complex organisms could devolve into simpler forms or animals.

Ray Lankester

The best technology has personality

That's why some products become design classics like the Volkswagen Beetle, the angle poise lamp or Philippe Starck's iconic lemon squeezer, The Juicy Salif shown here. Its combination of his personal obsessions – animal anatomy, space rockets and aluminium – made it original and unique. What are your three strongest design influences? Use them to inspire a cheese grater design.

I don't design clothes,
I design dreams.

Ralph Lauren

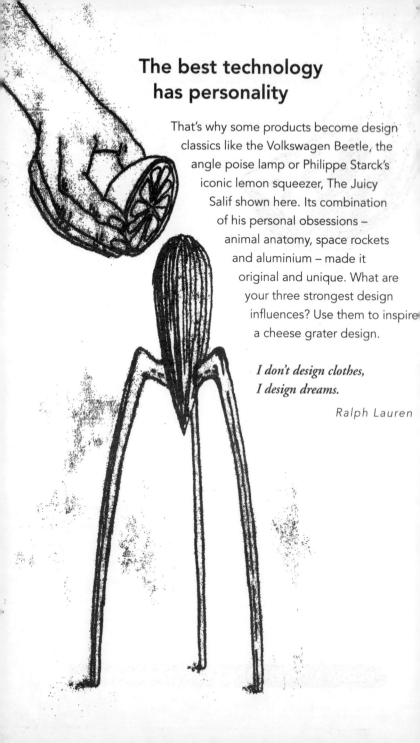

DESIGN A CHEESE GRATER WITH PERSONALITY

In design, new ideas always confront old formats

A coat of arms was an ancient way of identifying a family. In the twelfth century a knight dressed in armour was only recognizable by the symbols on his shield which described his background and tenets. They're still designed today. Bill Gates represents new technology and he needs a coat of arms.

Many people mistakenly think a new technology cancels out an old one.

Judith Martin

DESIGN A COAT OF ARMS FOR BILL GATES

What does the Internet look like?

The Stars and Stripes symbolize America. Fifty stars represent fifty states and thirteen stripes the first colonies of the union. Flags identify a geographical region but cyberspace is a new kind of territory – a vast digital universe filled with infinite constellations of data, a nexus of telecommunications networks. The virtual world of the Internet is an electronic space of no substance but unimaginable complexity.

Technology is the knack of so arranging the world that we don't have to experience it.

Max Frisch

DESIGN A FLAG FOR CYBERSPACE

Can design be so bad it's good?

The prolific British inventor Arthur Pedrick is a cult figure, revered by designers because none of his impractical devices worked or were ever commercially available. Bursting with ideas, he filed a record 162 patents for an individual before he died. Their total failure never dimmed his enthusiasm. A nuclear cat flap? An underwater bicycle? Steerable golf balls? Ideas so awful they were awesome. Celebrate his attributes with a monument.

Success consists of going from failure to failure without loss of enthusiasm.

Winston Churchill

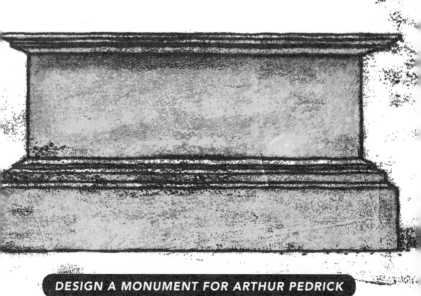

DESIGN A MONUMENT FOR ARTHUR PEDRICK

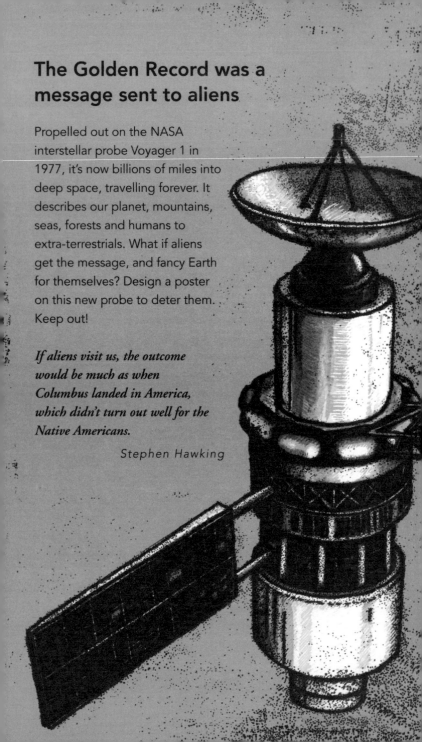

The Golden Record was a message sent to aliens

Propelled out on the NASA interstellar probe Voyager 1 in 1977, it's now billions of miles into deep space, travelling forever. It describes our planet, mountains, seas, forests and humans to extra-terrestrials. What if aliens get the message, and fancy Earth for themselves? Design a poster on this new probe to deter them. Keep out!

If aliens visit us, the outcome would be much as when Columbus landed in America, which didn't turn out well for the Native Americans.

Stephen Hawking

DESIGN A POSTER TO STOP ALIENS WANTING TO VISIT THE EARTH

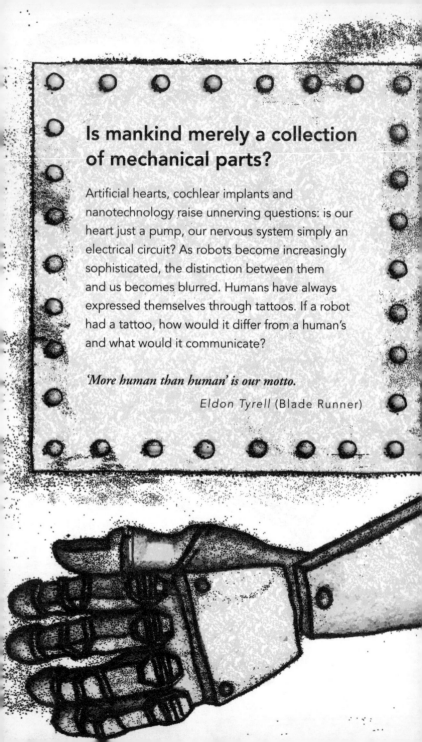

Is mankind merely a collection of mechanical parts?

Artificial hearts, cochlear implants and nanotechnology raise unnerving questions: is our heart just a pump, our nervous system simply an electrical circuit? As robots become increasingly sophisticated, the distinction between them and us becomes blurred. Humans have always expressed themselves through tattoos. If a robot had a tattoo, how would it differ from a human's and what would it communicate?

'More human than human' is our motto.

Eldon Tyrell (Blade Runner)

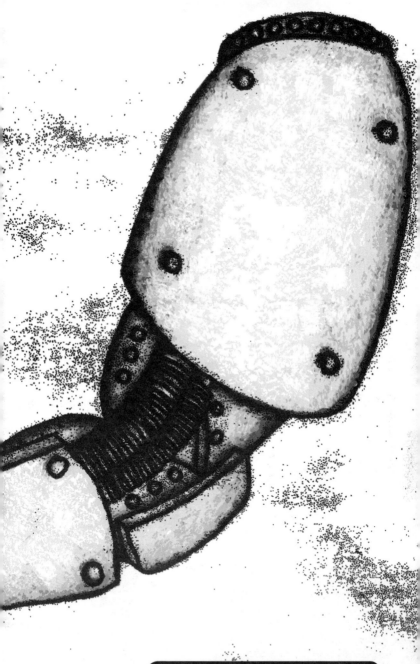

DESIGN A TATTOO FOR A ROBOT

Does technology control us rather than serve us?

Throughout history there have been those who embraced new technology and those who felt threatened by it. The Luddites of the nineteenth century resisted technological change because it led to job losses; others have complained that technology is the cause of modern man's sense of unease and alienation. Which modern technology do you dislike most and which would you want to see banned? Animated electronic billboards? Surveillance cameras? Ringtones? Imagine you're joining an anti-technology protest to parliament. Design your placard. Convey your anger.

The real danger is not that computers will begin to think like men, but that men will begin to think like computers.

Sydney J. Harris

'We declare… a new beauty, the beauty of speed,' proclaimed the Futurists

In a culture obsessed with acceleration, speed is an end in itself. If you're not fast then you must at least look fast. We know a parked Ferrari is quick because the sleek contours shout 'speed'. Nike trainers have sweeping curves and aerodynamic slashes. Cycle helmets have an undulating surface and swooping grooves. Design supersonic shells for the tortoise and snail that declare 'Fast forward into the future!'

The computer allows me to execute my ideas at the speed I think them.

Will.i.am

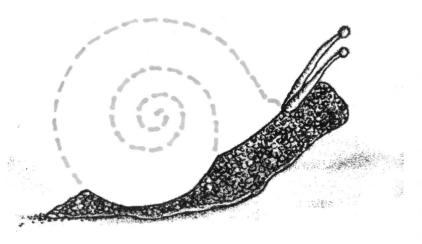

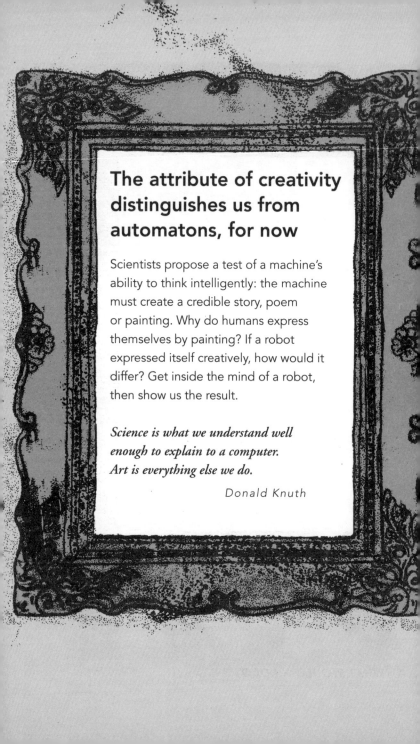

The attribute of creativity distinguishes us from automatons, for now

Scientists propose a test of a machine's ability to think intelligently: the machine must create a credible story, poem or painting. Why do humans express themselves by painting? If a robot expressed itself creatively, how would it differ? Get inside the mind of a robot, then show us the result.

Science is what we understand well enough to explain to a computer. Art is everything else we do.

Donald Knuth

WHAT WOULD A ROBOT'S PAINTING LOOK LIKE?

Are you on time?

Are you always racing against time? Are deadlines looming? Are you swept along by events? It's time you took stock of time: how you think about it, what you do with it and how you use it. You can't change chronological time but you can alter the way you work with it.

In multi-tasking overdrive, we frenetically try to save time and cram as much into the 1,440 minutes of the day as we can. It's a valuable commodity we're charged for, so we fill our world with time-saving devices: instant coffee, faster broadband, faster cars and faster trains. Faster, faster, faster. Everything is speeding up but paradoxically there's less time than ever. No matter how fast we live, we'll never have enough time for the ever-multiplying options now on offer to us – more and more films, TV shows, holiday destinations, sporting events, devices, apps and shortcuts. New activities and entertainments increase but your time remains limited.

Miklos Radnóti showed us how to use our time wisely. In 1944, a captive of the Nazi's, he knew he would soon be shot for being Jewish. He wrote a series of poems in a notebook before he was murdered and buried. His wife later had his body exhumed from a mass grave and the notebook was discovered in his pocket. It contained numerous extraordinary poems. He wrote, 'The pressure of time, the fact of mortality, the real deadline, compels me to create, and to create with awareness and intention.' How can *you* create and develop the ability to use time effectively?

The only reason for time is so that everything doesn't happen at once.

Albert Einstein

Will the universe end with a bang?

No. Scientists believe it will end in twenty-two billion years with a whimper. Atoms will simply drift apart. Boring. Design a firework to be let off seconds before the universe ends. It'll be a celebration of everything that's ever happened: champagne supernovas, C-beams glittering in the dark near the Tannhäuser Gate, Tunnock's Tea Cakes and supermassive quasars sucked into black holes. Firework designs reflect their exciting names: Nuclear Sunrise, Golden Shower, Confetti Cannon and Crackling Comet. What's yours called?

What the caterpillar calls the end of the world,
the Master calls the butterfly.

Richard Bach

DESIGN A FIREWORK FOR THE END OF THE UNIVERSE

Presents to die for

If you're visiting someone who is about to die, a bunch of flowers doesn't quite do it. It's their last few moments and it's down to you to make it meaningful.

Time is the most precious gift you can give to someone, because if you give someone your time, it's a part of your life that you will never get back.

Gloria Tesch

Time is money, so there is a new currency: sweat

You can only get rich
by labouring hard and
collecting your sweat.
The harder you toil,
the richer you become.
Design three containers,
small, medium and large,
for trading your sweat.

*It is well enough that
people of the nation
do not understand our
banking and monetary
system, for if they did,
I believe there would
be a revolution before
tomorrow morning.*

Henry Ford

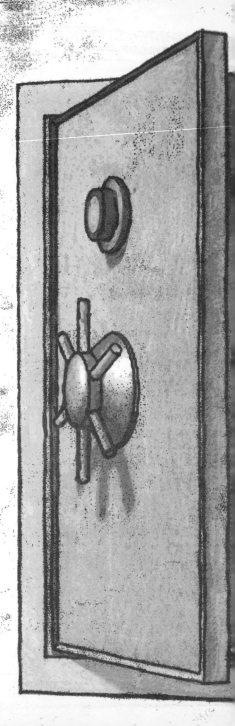

How does time feel to you?

A watch makes invisible time visible. It's a statement about how the owner thinks about time and it projects their personality. Do you see time as profound, ridiculous, muddled or in some other way?

A watch, it's a sign of the times.

Jarod Kintz

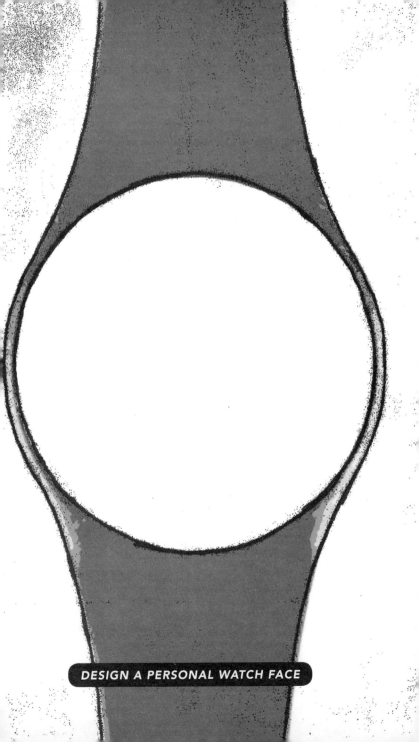

DESIGN A PERSONAL WATCH FACE

Can You call on Time?

The Earth rotating the Sun in twenty-four hours dictates our perceptio
of time. We'll need a new universal timescale when we settle on othe
planets. Design a clock for this mantelpiece on Nebula 6.

*Clock measurement is not time itself. In fact, so opposed are they that
one could argue the clock is not a synonym, but the opposite of time.*

Jay Griffith

What should endlessness look like?

Infinity inspires awe and astonishment. Everyone has looked up at the night sky and been dumbstruck by the apparently endless universe. A couple of loops (the current sign) hardly convey boundlessness. Summarize the essence of infinity; capture its immensity and wonder.

What does culture want? To make infinity comprehensible.

Umberto Eco

DESIGN AN INFINITY SYMBOL

Be thrilled by Einstein

A shocking thriller, revealing the most famous scientific concept of all time, Einstein's *Relativity: The Special and General Theory* proved time was no longer absolute. It could be speeded up or slowed down by dramatically strong forces. It anticipated time travel, black holes and The Big Bang Theory. It's mistakenly presented as a dreary science book when it's a heart-pounding adrenaline rush, full of mystery, suspense and surprise. Your cover must put it into the thriller section where it belongs.

Einstein, in the special theory of relativity, proved that different observers, in different states of motion, see different realities.

Leonard Susskind

Wallpaper is never purely decorative

It contains ideas; even a floral pattern expresses a notion, concept or judgement about nature. Artist Ai Weiwei's wallpaper depicted a pattern of security cameras linked by gold chains that allude to his confinement by the Chinese government. Artist Virgil Marti's wallpaper, Bullies, featured yearbook portraits of all the boys he was bullied by at junior high school. Think carefully about your wallpaper: it will be the only sight seen by the prisoner for weeks, months or even years.

This wallpaper is dreadful, one of us will have to go.

Oscar Wilde

DESIGN WALLPAPER FOR A SOLITARY CONFINEMENT CELL

How do you end the end?

Star Trek creator Gene Roddenberry's ashes were dispersed into outer space. Writer Hunter S Thompson's were fired from a cannon. Marvel Comics editor Mark Gruenwald's were blended with ink (most ancient inks were made from the ashes of corpses) and used to print a comic book. Guitarist Keith Richards added his father's ashes to cocaine and snorted them. Fredric Baur, inventor of the Pringles can, had his ashes buried in one. Decide which famous person's ashes are in the urn and do a drawing that describes a fitting end for them.

I also remember being struck by de Sade's will, in which he asked that his ashes be scattered to the four corners of the earth in the hope that humankind would forget both his writings and his name.

Luis Buñuel

Wormhole trips – book now

The theory of relativity predicted the existence of wormholes – tunnels through spacetime (or Einstein-Rosen Bridge) that make time travel possible. This shuttle flies down wormholes and the travel agency that runs it needs an aircraft livery, (the paint scheme, name and logo) to promote its brand. Arrive before you leave!

If time travel is possible, where are all the tourists from the future?

Stephen Hawking

DESIGN A SPACE TRAVEL AGENCY'S LIVERY

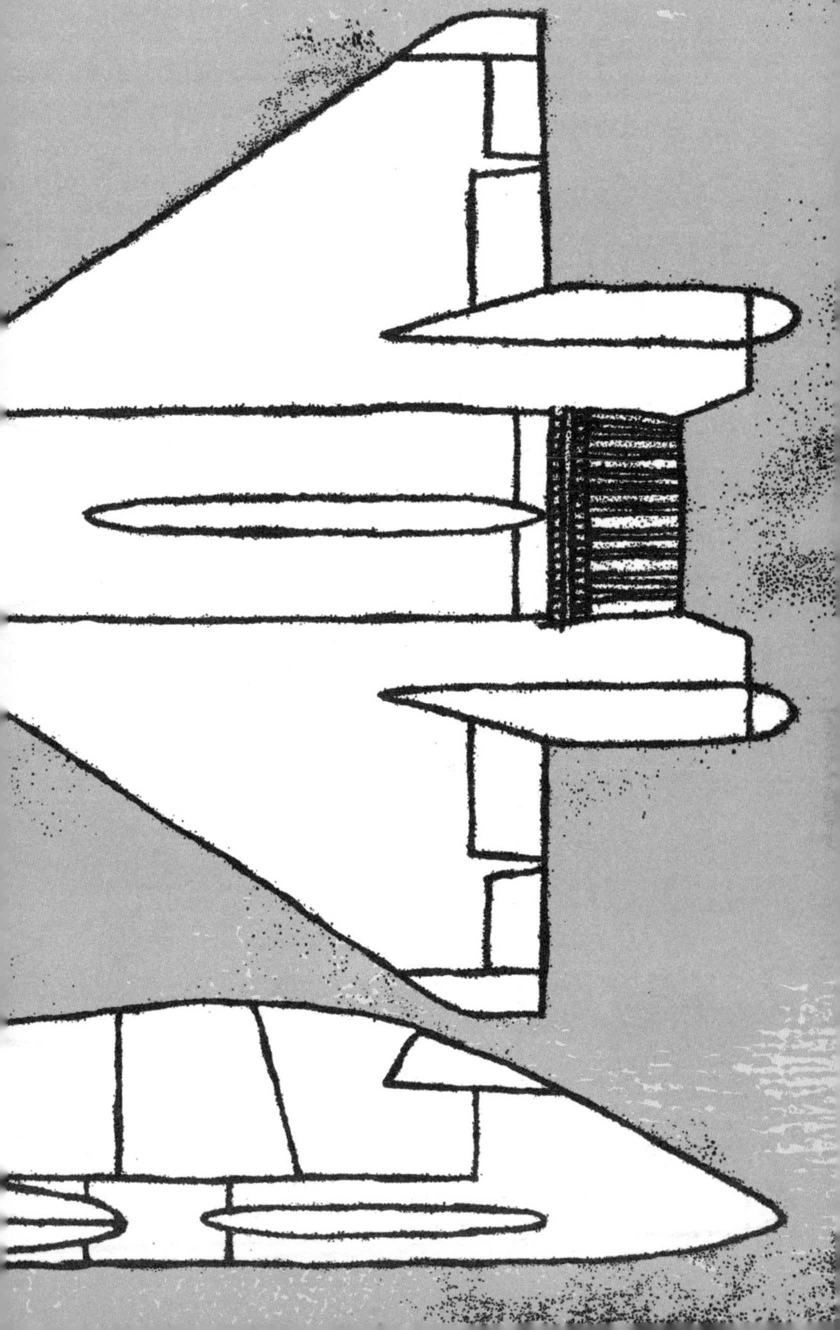

Are you an extremist?

Are you rich? If not, you must be poor. Are you happy? If not, you must be sad. Our sensationalist society polarizes people and events. Everything is exaggerated and extreme. This feeds through to us and we begin to think in extremes without even realizing it.

Binary oppositions are concepts with opposite meanings – up and down, good and bad. They organize our thoughts. 'Good' makes no sense without knowing what is 'bad.' If you explore a concept's opposite and understand what it is not, it's easier to understand what it is. The consequences are that our thinking becomes limited. We see everything as black or white and fail to notice the complexity and multiple shades of grey in between. This explains why our perception and understanding become increasingly restricted during a period of great technological advance.

Juxtaposition of opposites is one of the major characteristics of our culture and explains why many have failed to expand their consciousness and further their understanding. This chapter will help you be aware of those limitations in order to progress beyond them.

Our age knows nothing but reaction, and
leaps from one extreme to another.

Reinhold Niebuhr

Hamster from Hell

Imagine you are a genetic engineer, a designer of life. They use biotechnology to take DNA from one organism and add it to another. Their results: a genetically modified salmon to grow twice as fast. A sheep with added worm genes to make its meat lean and less fatty. A mouse that can chirp like a bird. Fluorescent rats that glow green in the dark, due to jelly fish genes. Pigs with human hearts that can be transplanted into people.

Hamsters are fluffy and useless. Splice one's genes with those of another animal to make it history's first extreme hamster.

With the advent of genetic engineering the time required for the evolution of a new species may literally collapse.

Dee Hock

CREATE AN EXTREME HAMSTER

Your rule is – no rules

A disaster for architecture, the Bauhaus insisted on straight lines, angles and squares. They're the reason our cities are a mass of alienating boxes. What the Bauhaus lacked in talent they made up for with rules. Reduce everything to basic geometric shapes! Form must follow function! Rules, rules, rules! They even made rules about the design of knives and forks. Take the Bau out of this haus by adding playful decorations to this building.

The life of a designer is a life of fight. Fight against the ugliness. Just like a doctor fights against disease.

Massimo Vignelli

Chairs aren't just places to sit

They convey social meaning through the symbols, patterns and texture of their fabric. One of these chairs belongs to the CEO of a global bank. The other belongs to one of its borrowers. Create different fabric designs that comment on their ranking.

Where there is power, there is resistance.

Michel Foucault

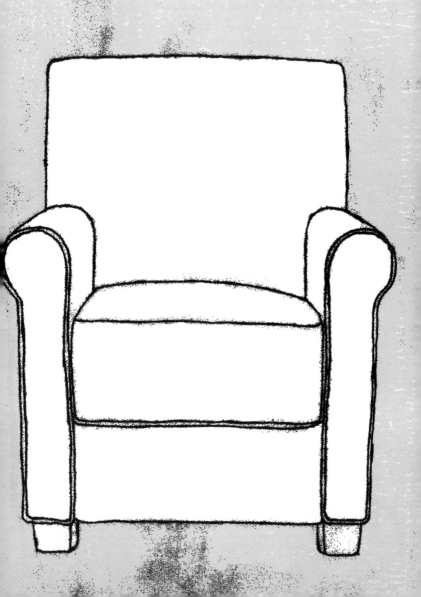

DESIGN THE FABRIC FOR THESE CHAIRS

Mind the Gap

One second you're in Europe, the next in Asia. Your bridge spans the Bosphorus Strait and links the West side to the Eastern side. How will your design reflect Western culture? Eastern culture? The merging of the two?

The real war is not between the West and the East. The real war is between intelligent and stupid people.

Marjane Satrapi

The Odd Couple

'Apollonian' and 'Dionysian' are terms Nietzsche took from Greek mythology to highlight two opposing traits in modern man. Apollo was the Greek god of reason and the rational. Dionysus was the god of chaos and the irrational. A Dyonisian is marrying an Apollonian. Celebrate their union in the design of their wedding cake.

What good is the warmth of summer, without the cold of winter to give it sweetness.

John Steinbeck

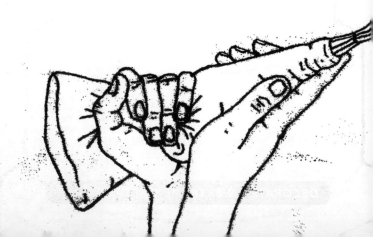

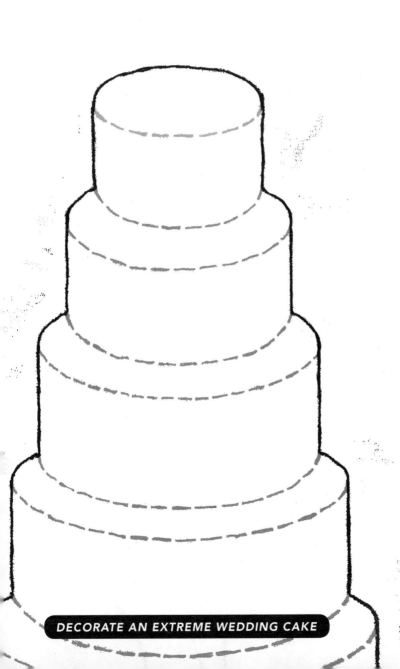

DECORATE AN EXTREME WEDDING CAKE

Hide a bear in McDonald's?

Camouflage enables animals to blend into their environment, forests, grasslands or deserts. Bears, foxes and other animals are now invading the city. Design camouflage for a metropolitan bear. The grey camouflage under these words was designed for soldiers in urban warfare. Be more imaginative.

I went to buy some camouflage trousers the other day but I couldn't find any.

Tommy Cooper

DESIGN CAMOUFLAGE FOR AN URBAN ANIMAL

Can a gun be beautiful?

Ray gun design is a strange mixture of beauty and aggression: the aesthetization of violence. Design is seen as a force for good, guns for bad. The ray gun throws imagination and future-gazing into the mix. Put a sci fi blaster in this hand that is as beautifully evil as Rick Deckard's blaster in *Blade Runner* or the iconic phasers from Star Trek.

'Make it evil,' he'd been told. 'Make it totally clear
that this gun has a right end and a wrong end.'

Douglas Adams

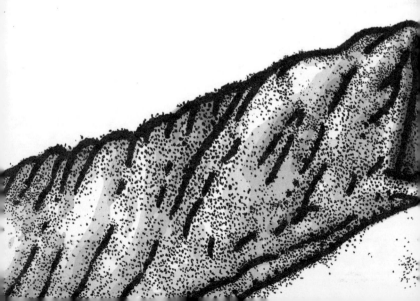

Roman prostitutes were great at advertising

They had the words 'follow me' imprinted on the soles of their sandals. As they walked they left a trail for a customer to follow. Design a shoe tread with a message from a contemporary sinner.

The more I had to act like a saint, the more I felt like being a sinner.

Max von Sydow

DESIGN A SHOE TREAD FOR A MODERN SINNER

Does Your Hair Talk?

Draw a side parting and cropped moustache on a photo of anyone and they're transformed into Hitler. A savagely cut back-and-sides with a long black slash of hair looks brutal and autocratic. Hitler deliberately constructed an iconic look, now synonymous with Fascism, to make him instantly recognizable. Where's the immediately identifiable pacifist style? Create an iconic anti-fascist haircut.

Hair brings one's self-image into focus; it is vanity's proving ground.

Shana Alexander

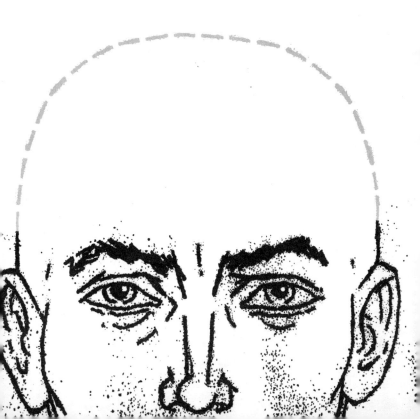

You gotta say yes to another excess

The Body is a Battleground. It's a medium of expression for a diet and physique-obsessed society. The obese rebel against the body ideals forced on us: Screw you! I won't live up to your standards! The deep-fried Mars Bar has become a symbol for ill health and overindulgence. It's a Mars Bar, covered in batter and deep-fried. Design a billboard to persuade people it's good to be bad.

I don't stop eating when I'm full.
The meal isn't over when I'm full.
It's over when I hate myself.

Louis CK

ADVERTISE DEEP-FRIED MARS BARS

Are you in control?

Are you free? How much power do you have? We have all felt powerless. A woman sitting in front of an interview panel full of men or a child in a principal's office knows what it's like to feel vulnerable. How do we gain more control over our lives?

We are all like Truman Burbank in the film *The Truman Show*. He's the star of a TV soap opera and lives in a giant studio, the invention of a television station. Thousands of cameras film everything he does, twenty-four hours a day. But he doesn't know. Truman grew up in the programme and although everyone around him is an actor, everything seems completely real to him. He lives in a world in which newspapers, television and radio are fictional inventions whose sole purpose is to deceive him. He comes to suspect that everything is being staged and eventually breaks free. It's a metaphor for how we live now. The consumer society shapes our lives, forms our views, and saturates us with stories. A single newspaper today contains more information than a person in the seventeenth century came across in their entire life. We need to be conscious of the many sources influencing our ideas. If we're not thinking for ourselves, asserting our own autonomy and taking control of our own lives, how can we ever be free?

Power is everywhere…and comes from everywhere.

Michel Foucault

Who's in charge?

Playing cards are a great example of symmetry. A card can't be held upside down. The King, Queen, Jack and Joker are based on the ancient hierarchy of a monarchy. Design a set of cards to represent the modern equivalent as you see it: a contemporary hierarchy of who is really in charge.

In a hierarchy, every employee tends to rise to his level of incompetence.

Laurence J Peter

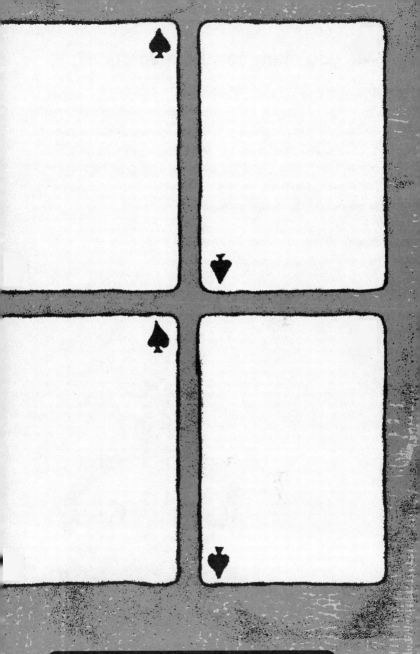

DESIGN CONTEMPORARY PLAYING CARDS

Are you ready for the revolution?

The crown symbolized the authority of an all-powerful monarch. That was in ancient times, but then Communism aimed to return authority to the people. Communist presidents publicly reject the pomp and pomposity of monarchy, yet privately own fleets of Ferrari's, Mailbu mansions, personal zoos, gold bathtubs and jewel-encrusted guns. Highlight the hypocrisy of communist presidents in the design for their crown.

Nearly all men can stand adversity, but if you want to test a man's character, give him power.

Abraham Lincoln

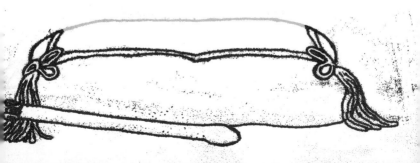

We are the champions

An iconic person is venerated because they symbolize a philosophy. An iconoclast is a person who attacks and destroys icons. A game of football has been arranged between the two sides. Design their strips.

The history of art is the history of iconoclasm, the history of some new voice saying that everything you know is wrong.

Richard Powers

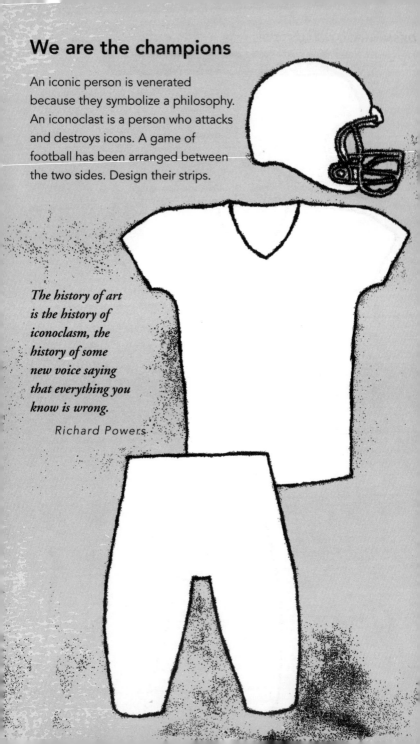

I predict a riot

A Molotov Cocktail is an empty bottle filled with petrol. A wick is inserted, lit, and the bottle is thrown. It smashes on impact, causing a fireball. Design the label and brand look for a new pre-mixed cocktail of the same name that's also a bomb (alcohol is flammable). Sipping a Molotov at a bar when a riot kicks off? Tear the label from the bottle, push it into the neck, ignite and take control.

The revolution is not an apple that falls when it's ripe. You have to make it fall.

Che Guevara

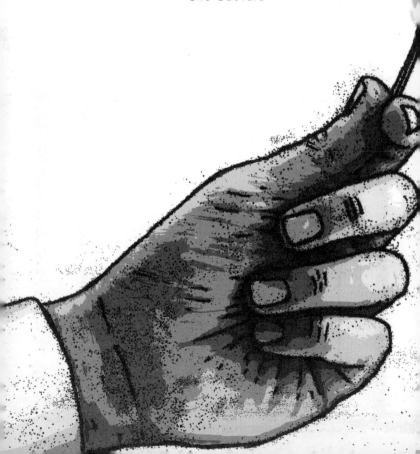

Every seventh one's a freebie

Loyalty cards are a powerful emotional weapon in a brand's armament over a customer. Cool, eye-catching designs hook and then trap a client. Prostitutes' customers aren't reliable. Change that with the design of a card and the stamps. Six visits and the seventh is free.

I believe that sex is one of the most beautiful, natural, wholesome things that money can buy.

Steve Martin

DESIGN A LOYALTY CARD FOR A PROSTITUTE

Wish You Were Here

Utopia is the perfect, ideal society. Everyone is happy with the faultless political system. We send postcards to show people what the place we've travelled to is like. Design one for what you think would be the perfect future city.

Utopian visions provide an ideal which people can then struggle to reach.

Erin McKenna

Own the sky

Medieval cathedrals towered over the city. Their flying buttresses and soaring vertical interiors with ribbed vaults were awe-inspiring. People flocked to them in droves but now they're empty. The people won't come to the cathedral so take it to them, wherever they are. We have inflatable swimming pools, bouncy castles and boats. Design a contemporary, inflatable cathedral that doesn't take itself too seriously but draws people together and fills them with wonder again.

Mankind was never so happily inspired
as when it made a cathedral.

Robert Louis Stevenson

It would destroy civilization as we know it

The single, all-destructive button has cultural resonance. It's a metaphor for the machine age's ability to place godlike power in the fingers of ethical infants. Many countries have a nuclear button. They all look the same. No gravitas, no sense of importance, just an ordinary red button. Convey messages fit for the occasion by designing a button using shape, wording or imagery.

Now, I am become Death, the destroyer of worlds.

J Robert Oppenheimer

What event should be recorded for posterity?

Archaeologists have a detailed account of momentous events in ancient Egypt from the illustrations on their walls. We gain a deeper understanding of a culture from the historical events they decide to record. Continue this freeze to explain an important event from modern culture to future archaeologists. Keep to the Egyptian style.

Archaeology is the search for fact... not truth. If it's truth you're looking for, Dr. Tyree's philosophy class is right down the hall.

Indiana Jones

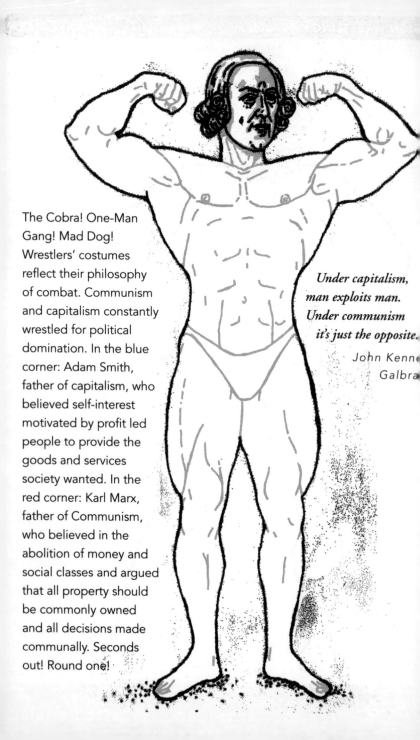

The Cobra! One-Man Gang! Mad Dog! Wrestlers' costumes reflect their philosophy of combat. Communism and capitalism constantly wrestled for political domination. In the blue corner: Adam Smith, father of capitalism, who believed self-interest motivated by profit led people to provide the goods and services society wanted. In the red corner: Karl Marx, father of Communism, who believed in the abolition of money and social classes and argued that all property should be commonly owned and all decisions made communally. Seconds out! Round one!

Under capitalism, man exploits man. Under communism it's just the opposite.

John Kenne
Galbra

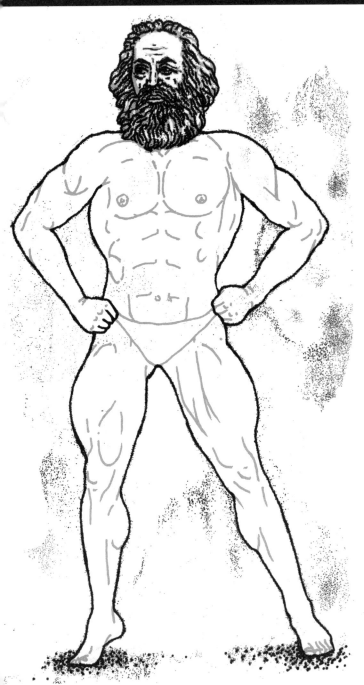

Are you the future?

What will you be doing in the future? What do you want the future to be like? The future's important because you're going to end up there. You are going to either shape it or be shaped by it.

It's human nature to anticipate what is beyond the horizon. The cars, buildings and computers of tomorrow are in the heads of dreamers and designers right now. These visionaries are striding into the future while others are content to sit in the past. They imagine what they want the future to be and then create it. They strive to improve, to make things better. Architects want better buildings, vehicle designers want better cars and fashion designers want improved clothing. The creative think about what could be. Why design a new chair? There are hundreds of thousands of chair designs. But the designer thinks he can do better, come up with a new idea. Design is more than simply future forecasting or problem-solving – it transforms imagination into reality. What is *your* contribution to improving the future? Do you want to take part or sit on the sidelines?

If you work out where your culture is going, you can help to steer it.

Take hold of the future or the future will take hold of you.

Patrick Dixon

Is it normal to be unnatural?

Commemorative flowers memorialize someone. The poppy honours fallen soldiers. After Princess Diana's death, a rose was designed to celebrate her. Many scientists now believe we are slowly killing nature. We've 'paved over paradise'. We replace real lawns with plastic ones, real flowers for fake, and clear Amazon rainforests. Design a flower that commemorates the death of nature.

My fake plants died because I did not pretend to water them.

Mitch Hedberg

Jules Verne invented the future

A science fiction writer in the early nineteenth century, Verne predicted the submarine, spaceflight, solar panels, video conferencing, the Taser gun and much more. Design a commemorative plaque (a permanent sign installed in a public place) for someone alive today who is inventing the future.

The great person is ahead of their time, the smart make something out of it, and the blockhead sets themselves against it.

Jean Baudrillard

Shock the neighbours

The past is often the key to the future. The small, ornamental humanoid creatures wearing pointed hats that plague suburban gardens with saccharine cuteness are descended from the Greco-Roman fertility god Priapus. In Roman times they were mischievous creatures of the Underworld with macro phalluses. Rock suburbia! Modernize them and reinstate the fertility theme.

Sex is part of nature. I go along with nature.

Marilyn Monroe

Take it out on a piece of wood

Its origins are lost in the mist of time. Today's chess set is based on medieval warfare. The pawns represent serfs – cannon fodder – the castle protection and the bishop, the power of religion. The knight is represented by the mobility of his horse. The queen dominates the boa due to her versatility but the king was the kingdom's most important person. Design a chess set that reflects the hierarchy of modern warfar

The real trouble with war (modern war) is that it gives no one a chance to kill the right people.

Ezra Pound

King   Queen   Bishop

Knight   Castle   Pawn

If only God would give me some clear sign! Like making a large deposit in my name at a Swiss bank.

Woody Allen

Coming to your high street

– between the bank and the dry cleaner – a money laundering service. Keep clear of the regulators! Leave your dirty, corrupt money to be washed through off-shore bank accounts via the Internet and collect the legit notes a few hours later. Design the front of the shop and window display – what's it called?

55

DESIGN A MONEY LAUNDERING SHOP

Create a nuclear dustbin

Architects rarely design a building to last longer than a hundred years. A nuclear waste storage facility must never require maintenance and cannot be opened for 10,000 years. It must be more durable than anything we ever build and could be humankind's legacy. It will outlive our language and symbols. The shape of the building alone must speak to those in the future and say 'Stay away, extreme danger.'

The discovery of nuclear chain reactions need not bring about the destruction of mankind any more than did the discovery of matches. We must do everything in our power to safeguard against its abuse.

Albert Einstein

DESIGN A NUCLEAR WASTE FACILITY

Packaging for a turkey baster

Artificial insemination is a commercial business. Women can buy the donated genes of successful scientists, writers, musicians and sportsmen. Whose genes do you think should be passed on? Each insemination package in this vending machine has a picture of the donor on the cover. Draw in the faces of those you think should form the next generation.

We have decommissioned natural selection and must now look deep within ourselves and decide what we wish to become.

EO Wilson

DESIGN SPERM DONOR PACKETS

Customize your paradise

'The gates of paradise' is how Michelangelo referred to Lorenzo Ghiberti's fifteenth-century doors for the Baptistery of St John, Florence. The gilded panels depicted scenes from the Bible decorated by a framework of foliage and fruit. But what would a future idea of paradise be?

An intelligent hell would be better than a stupid paradise.

Victor Hugo

What was this Victorian utensil used for?

No one knows. It's obsolete. Planned obsolescence is designing a product with a deliberately limited life. Future-proofing is the opposite: the process of anticipating the future and developing products that adapt to changes in the market. Revive this object. Add elements to future-proof it, ensuring it will be endlessly useful and fashionable.

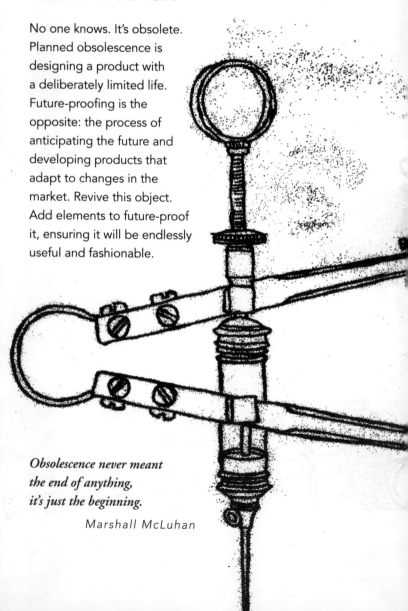

Obsolescence never meant the end of anything, it's just the beginning.

Marshall McLuhan

Retro refit the ultimate eco vehicle, the mule

To make Ferrari drivers jealous, it will need to be pimped up: restored, customized and massively and ridiculously upgraded. Designers always look back to the past to create the future. They take the best and improve the worst. Add an amazing saddle, headgear or sound system?

Nostalgia is a vey complicated subject for me. I'm attracted by nostalgia but I refuse it intellectually.

Miuccia Prada

Are you *you*?

'Know yourself', said Socrates. But how can you know yourself when you are in yourself? You can never step 'outside' and be objective.

Are you your body or your mind? The incorporeal mind affects the physical body and vice versa. Biochemists have proved your body's hormones govern your mind, but your brain governs your body's nervous system.

Your body is a battleground where ideas of perfection and authenticity fight for supremacy, but these ideas change with time. In some eras it was fashionable to be thin, in others plump. A 'perfect body' in 1930 wouldn't be acceptable to model agencies today.

We've always been surrounded by images of idealized people. While in the past, few people could attain their flawless selves, now we can, thanks to new products to make our hair shinier, our skin faultless and surgical implants to transform us. There are pills to make you look younger, slimmer, lighter and darker, or to convert you in any way you choose. Gene therapy can improve you and surgery can modify you. This means more of us than ever can be satisfied with who we are and how we look. This chapter explores ideas about the modern body, how they shape you and your concept of yourself.

How have all these cultural ideas made you the person you are? If you're a work in progress, where are you progressing?

The chief function of the body is to carry the brain around.

Thomas Edison

Interrogate yourself

Danger: Excessively sarcastic! May cause drowsiness! Mouth operates faster than brain! Do not touch: hot surface! High noise level! Crumbles under pressure! Is there something toxic about you? Are some people allergic to you? Can you objectively identify your shortfalls in order to improve yourself? Be bluntly honest.

Your visions will become clear only when you can look into your own heart. Who looks outside, dreams; who looks inside, awakes.

CG Jung

IMAGINE YOU'RE A BOTTLE.
WHICH WARNINGS ARE ON YOUR LABEL?

How free are you?

Determinists believe an individual has no free will because we're puppets controlled by the values of society. They consider that our media culture dictates who we are and what we think. The individual carving his own destiny against an authoritarian power is a common theme of pinball machines: Luke Skywalker fighting the Empire or James Bond combating Spectre. You're the ball. Who is your adversary? Design your route to freedom.

The media's the most powerful entity on earth. They have the power to make the innocent guilty and to make the guilty innocent, and that's power.

Malcolm X

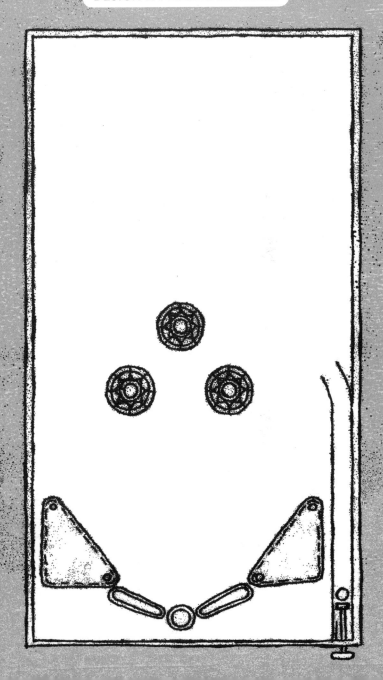

Oh, the cleverness of you

Vinyl dolls of rock, film and sports stars synthesize a personality down to its most obvious features. What is your most extreme characteristic? Create a vinyl doll that visualizes your defining trait.

We're only here once and I want to get as much out of it as possible. And as an artist, my job is to be as much 'me' as possible.

Grayson Perry

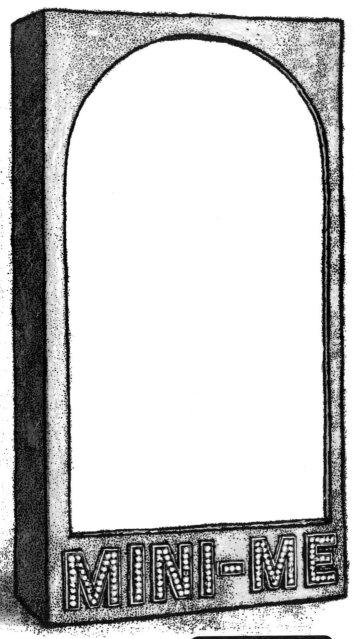

DESIGN A MINI-ME

Does society need superheroes?

Philosopher Friedrich Nietzsche believed so. Such heroes would rise above conventional morality and act as their own God. Imagine you're a superhero created to overthrow traditions. What conventions will you overturn? Design your costume and your sidekick's. Consider colours, capes, a signature letter (Superman had an 'S' logo, Spiderman a spider and Batman a bat logo), mask, utility belt and distinctive weapon.

What is great in man is that he is a bridge and not a goal.

Friedrich Nietzsche

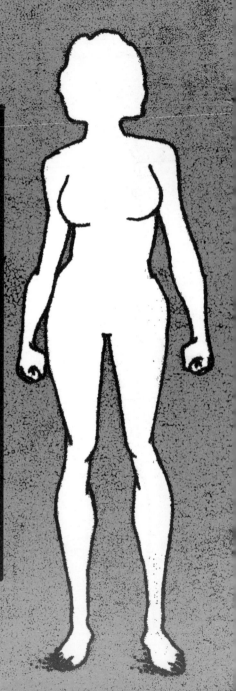

DESIGN A SUPERHERO COSTUME FOR YOURSELF

Does hero worship prevent you from becoming a hero in your own right?

It's time to stop looking up to an icon and look down on them. Desecrate your idol. Draw the face of the person you most admire on the urinal. For your own good it's time they were defiled.

Lou Reed was a hero because he was an anti-hero.

Tom Stoppard

DESTROY YOUR HERO

'Each of us constructs and lives a "narrative",' said neurologist Oliver Sacks

'This narrative is us'. We invent ourselves. Like novelists, we mix the fact and fiction of our lives and make them into a single story. 'The chief fictional character at the centre of that autobiography is one's self,' said philosopher Daniel Dennett. We become the story we tell about ourselves. Re-create an event from your past as a comic, then tell the same story from another person's point of view.

All autobiography is storytelling; all writing is autobiography.

J. M. Coetzee

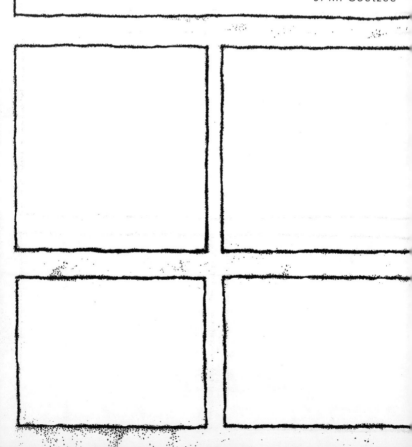

What's special about your body?

Medical museums ask people to donate part of their body to their collection when they die. What would you contribute and why? Design the display case to emphasize and communicate what's unique about your body part.

Our bodies are apt to be our autobiographies.

Frank Gillette Burgess

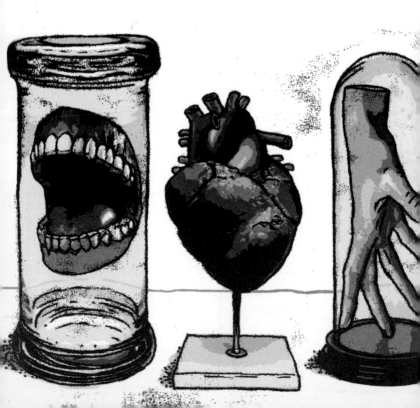

DONATE A PART OF YOUR BODY TO A MUSEUM

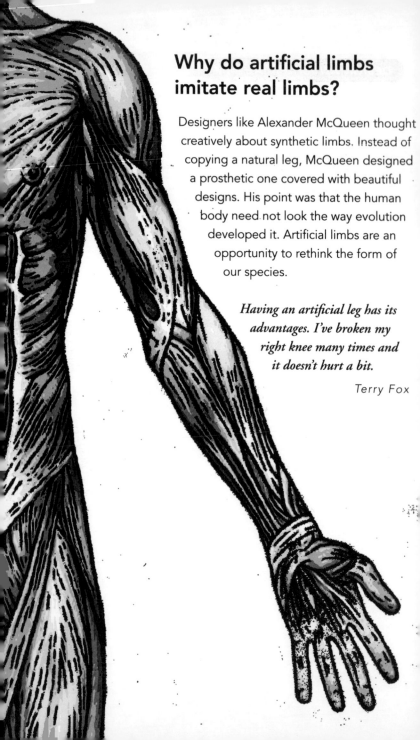

Why do artificial limbs imitate real limbs?

Designers like Alexander McQueen thought creatively about synthetic limbs. Instead of copying a natural leg, McQueen designed a prosthetic one covered with beautiful designs. His point was that the human body need not look the way evolution developed it. Artificial limbs are an opportunity to rethink the form of our species.

Having an artificial leg has its advantages. I've broken my right knee many times and it doesn't hurt a bit.

Terry Fox

DESIGN AN ARTIFICIAL ARM

Make a big impression

You leave your print on life everywhere you go via your fingerprints. You leave a trace on everything you touch. Fingerprint recognition ensures your fingerprints have a digital record on your devices. But a fingerprint is a swirl of meaningless lines. It's now possible to biohack fingerprints, either with customized skin grafts or genetic alterations. Re-design your fingerprint. Leave a message, either with imagery or words.

Values are like fingerprints. Nobody's are the same, but you leave them all over everything you do.

Elvis Presley

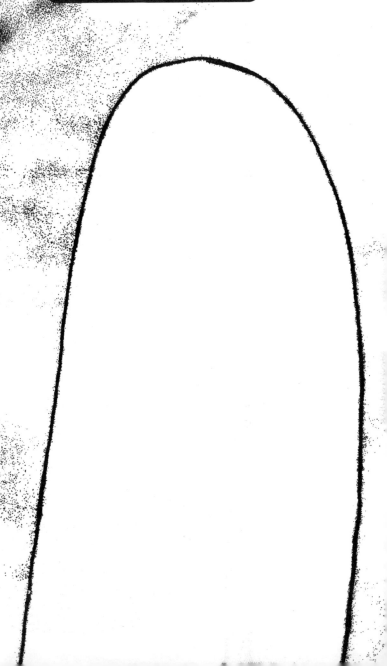

Want a diploma?

Saul Steinberg's friend Charles Eames, studied architecture in Germany for seven years. The Nazis refused to award his qualification because he was Jewish. So Steinberg designed a diploma and awarded it to Eames. He mimicked the neurotically intricate patterns, ostentatious signatures and posturing insignia. What do you deserve a diploma for? Design your diploma. Mock the overinflated flamboyance and pomposity of authority.

I don't deserve this award, but I have arthritis and I don't deserve that either.

Jack Benny

This is to certify that

AWARD YOURSELF A DIPLOMA

Are you for real?

What is real? Money? Work? Love? How do you know they're real? Perhaps they're complicated creations of your own mind. We take reality for granted because it physically always seems to be there. Great thinkers from Plato to Stephen Hawking seem more uncertain about reality than lesser minds. Are you sure the colours you're seeing now are out there in the real world or a perception created by your mind? And then there are the building blocks of reality, atomic particles, which we can't even see and lead us into the bizarre world of quantum mechanics and string theory. Matter itself begins to seem ethereal and conceptual.

If you don't understand the world around you, how can you even begin to do anything? Our social world has been created by the consumer society. How can you communicate what you think without a deep understanding of how advertising companies and governments have shaped your thoughts? You may think you know what's real and what isn't, but the more reality is probed the more it isn't what it seems. What we believe rarely relates to the fundamentals of truth, knowledge or reality. We must relentlessly question 'why?' and dig down for the reality behind the illusions. Without understanding the world around us we can't meaningfully contribute to it.

Reality leaves a lot to the imagination.

John Lennon

I drink, therefore I am

The English coffee houses of the seventeenth century were set up to discuss serious philosophical and political matters. Unlike beer, coffee sharpened and focused the mind. A subversive alternative to the regulated atmosphere of universities, they are associated with the birth of The Age of Enlightenment when reason came to dominate thought. You've recreated one for the modern age. Declare its principles in the coffee cup design.

The idea of just wandering off to a café with a notebook and writing and seeing where that takes me for a while is just bliss.

JK Rowling

DESIGN A COFFEE CUP FOR A PHILOSOPHERS' CAFÉ

Why do scientists keep the best toys to themselves?

The Large Hadron Collider lies in a tunnel seventeen miles in circumference, six hundred feet beneath France and Switzerland. The particle accelerator is the largest machine in the world, and took thousands of scientist's decades to build. It pushes at the limits of scientific enquiry and reveals reality, the inner secrets of atoms. Miles of superconducting electromagnets chilled to 271.3°C recline in an ultra-high vacuum. The particles travel close to the speed of light before colliding. We want one!

If quantum mechanics hasn't profoundly shocked you, you haven't understood it yet.

Niels Bohr

We all have a public persona and a private self

Virtually everyone wears a mask to be accepted. Some people are so fake and insincere that their masks bear no relation whatsoever to what's beneath. Create a warning sticker to expose phonies.

To pretend, I actually do the thing: I have therefore only pretended to pretend.

Jacques Derrida

Postmodernists are unified by one belief

Namely, there cannot be a single, uniform belief. Postmodern philosophers declared metanarratives – broad, coherent ideologies such as Marxism, Feminism, Science, Capitalism and Religion – to be dead.

Greek philosophers wore flowing white robes. Existentialists wore black polo neck jumpers. Design a uniform for Postmodernists.

It is our virtue to be infinitely varied.
The worst tyranny is uniformity.

George William Russell

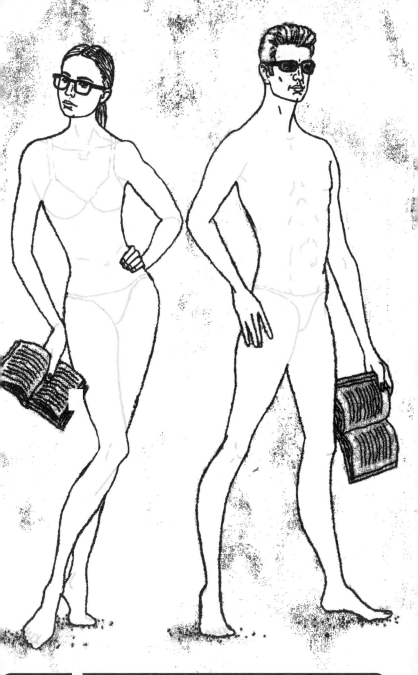

DESIGN A UNIFORM FOR A POSTMODERN PHILOSOPHER

We don't have to be our real selves

We can be transformed with pills that make us whiter, darker, slimmer, fatter, grow breasts, change gender, grow hair, and achieve erections. What would you alter about yourself? Design the packaging for your new pill, with the name and wrapping explaining and selling the product.

I re-invented my image so many times that I'm in denial that I was originally an overweight Korean woman.

David Bowie

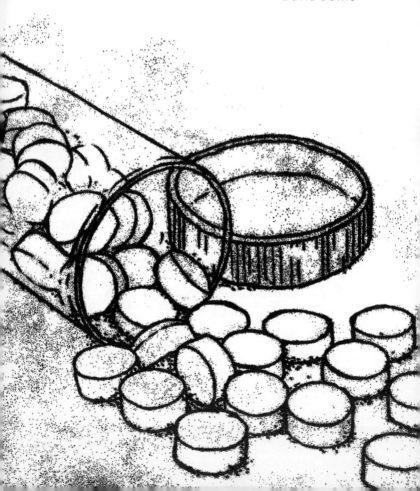

INVENT A NEW DRUG

Did you revere a childhood toy?

We've all encountered children who insist their plastic doll or soft teddy is real. But it's not just childish confusion: toys become real in our hearts and minds. It's one of the closest relationships we ever experience. Instead of throwing them out when they're old, bury them with respect. Tombs used to incorporate sculptures of the dead with inscriptions and ornamentation that explained why they were so unique and badly missed. Design a tomb for your favourite toy that conveys their irreplaceable attributes.

You're a toy! You aren't a real Buzz Lightyear.

Woody

You have to laugh...

What is it about the colours, make-up and design of a clown costume that signifies to people – get ready to laugh? The postmodern philosopher Jacques Derrida was fascinated by clown costumes like the Pierrot's. He analysed them to understand how the mere sight of them symbolized humour. He is best known for deconstruction, a way of intellectually dismantling something, piece by piece, to comprehend it better. Here's Jacques: design a costume for him that will trigger uncontrollable laughter.

The clown has great importance as part of the search for what is laughable and ridiculous in man.

Jacques Lecoq

DESIGN A CLOWN COSTUME FOR A PHILOSOPHER

What is the American Dream?

James Truslow Adams used the phrase to describe the ideal that equality of opportunity is available to everyone to achieve their highest goals. But it is different for every individual. What is yours? The pursuit of material prosperity, luxury cars and high earnings? A dream of social order and liberty? Living a simple, fulfilling life? What forces propel you to your goal? Go forward two squares. What obstacles hinder you? Go back one square. What is the end goal?

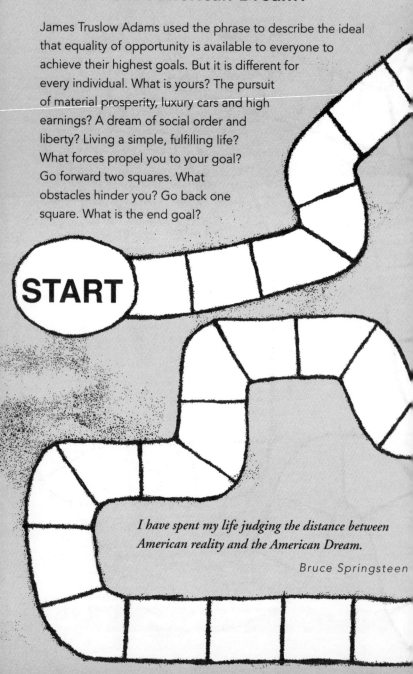

START

I have spent my life judging the distance between American reality and the American Dream.

Bruce Springsteen

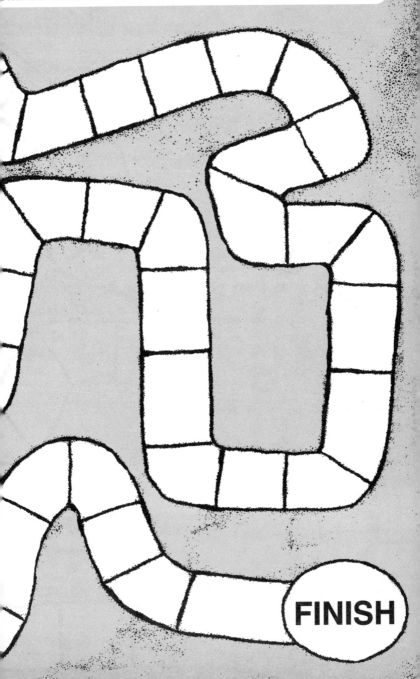

FINISH

You're surrounded by zombies

They're soulless, robotically driven former people. With deadpan expressions they commute to work like automata, sit in front of computer screens all day, then trudge home to mindlessly watch TV soaps and go online to take their consciousness offline. Wake them from their routines! Snap them back to reality! What utensils would a Zombie cure kit require?

Culture is just a shambling zombie that repeats what it did in life; bits drop off, and it doesn't appear to notice.

Alan Moore

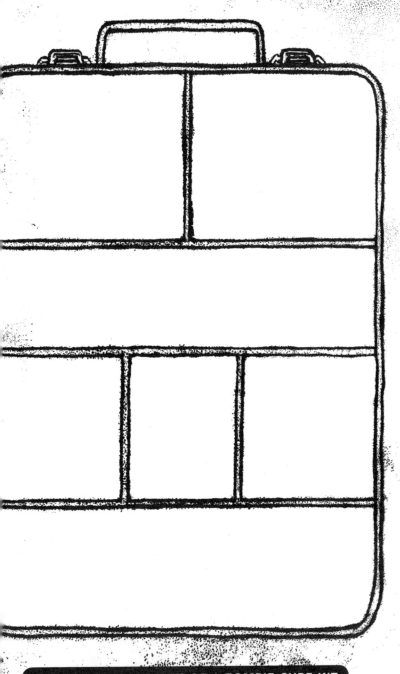

DESIGN THE CONTENTS OF A ZOMBIE CURE KIT

Set an imagination on fire

Our culture doesn't need any more firemen to put out fires, it needs firestarters to ignite metaphorical blazes, fire new ideas at people, throw light on reality, create heated debates, spark curiosity and create burning desires. Design the insignia and apparatus on their fire engine.

The mind is not a vessel to be filled but a fire to be kindled.

Plutarch

Are you valued?

Are you so busy with day-to-day life that you forget to evaluate whether you're putting your energy into the things you value most? The answer may be yes, but how do you decide what's valuable? And are your values yours, or your culture's?

Back in 450BC Protagoras highlighted a strikingly contemporary concept. There are no absolute values, he said: we each create our own. This is why we often hear the phrase 'That's true for you but not for me.' As well as being subjective, values are in a constant state of flux. In the blink of an eye, good can become bad and the worthless infinitely precious.

How do you determine value in a society that commodifies everything, in a culture in which we get richer and richer and simultaneously less and less happy? Economists distinguish between real and phantom wealth. Real wealth, such as knowledge, pure water, health, close families and safe neighbourhoods, has intrinsic value but no worldly price. Phantom wealth is the money Wall Street generates in astounding amounts with accounting tricks, market bubbles and snowballing debts.

The real world is full of compromise, and we constantly adjust our values to fit into it. What you define as important dictates your actions, and is a crucial step towards conducting life in a meaningful and satisfying way. The projects in this chapter will help you examine your values and question what really matters to you.

I think a power to do something is of value. Whether the result is a good thing or a bad thing depends on how it is used, but the power is a value.

Richard Feynman

The US Federal Reserve is the bank of banks

It supervises and regulates every other bank in the US. Money is power and the US is the richest nation on earth. If America sneezes, the world catches a cold. Decisions made in the Fed affect us all.

Above the door of the Fed stands an American eagle. Design a more appropriate statue.

Let me issue and control a nation's money and I care not who writes the laws.

Mayer Amschel Rothschild

FEDERAL RESERVE

Does money attract money?

With one spray of Cash anyone can be drenched in the odour of success. Smell rich with Cash – the fragrance. Reek of a million dollars, instantly, with no effort. The strong aroma of high cotton and silk content paper; the intense smell of engraving ink; the whiff of aluminium foil threads; all create the scent of a freshly printed dollar bill.

Could you sell this? What would you put on the label to persuade someone to buy it?

It's great to buy friends. I don't think there's anything wrong with having a lot of money and attracting people with it. Look who you're attracting: EVERYBODY!

Andy Warhol

CASH IS A NEW PERFUME. DESIGN THE LABEL

Consumerism is the new religion and shopping malls are the new temples

We flock to designer heaven and devote ourselves to salvation, not in the afterlife but in this life. Families used to pray together; now they pay together. For centuries, stained glass windows in cathedrals conveyed religious values to the masses. Capture the ideals of consumerism in this window, the centrepiece of a shopping mall.

We no longer live life. We consume it.

                                    Vicki Robin

ESIGN A STAINED GLASS WINDOW FOR A SHOPPING CENTRE

What do you think is your nation's greatest asset?

Banknotes are part of the fabric of daily life and therefore help to define the national identity. Designed by conservative committees of powerful establishment authorities, they supposedly reflect national values by celebrating great figures and institutions from the past. But they tend to feature solemn, bland, national clichés. Break conventions! You're a treasury designer; design a banknote for your country of origin capturing what you feel are its best values, no matter how subversive.

A weak currency is the sign of a weak economy, and a weak economy leads to a weak nation.

Ross Perot

Ignore the homeless

They often sit holding a sign stating a cliché like 'please give, homeless.' One sunny morning, on his way to work, an advertising copywriter passed a blind beggar whose sign read, 'I'M BLIND. PLEASE HELP.' The copywriter stopped, took out a marker pen, wrote three words on the sign and moved on. From then on the beggar's cup was stuffed with money. The adapted sign read: 'IT'S SPRING AND I'M BLIND. PLEASE HELP.'

How will you persuade passers-by to stop and give? With humour? Pity? Interactivity?

Seven out of ten Americans are one paycheck away from being homeless.

Pras Michel

Who Wants To Be A Millionaire?

In the American psyche Las Vegas is the spiritual home of gambling and capital city of risk-taking. It's capitalism distilled: an opulent paradise of exaggeration and excessiveness. A city with no past, appearing in the Nevada desert like an oasis, it's an adult playground packed with fruit machines, roulette wheels and blackjack tables. A bum can enter with a dollar and leave a millionaire or vice versa.

How risky – or risk-averse – are you? What's the message on your sign?

Life is either a daring adventure or nothing at all.

Helen Keller

RE-DESIGN THE LAS VEGAS WELCOME SIGN

'Failure is not an option'

This phrase became etched into our culture's success-driven minds when NASA declared it during the mission to return damaged Apollo 13 to Earth. Our most costly failure is our obsession with success. We are wrong about what it means to be wrong. The capacity to fail is crucial to development because it's life's greatest teacher. This is particularly true in business: entrepreneurs learn through failure, which in commercial terms means losing money, even going bankrupt. There are awards that celebrate every conceivable achievement, except failure.

Design a trophy for the person who has lost the most money this year. Who said not having money made you a loser?

Ever tried. Ever failed. No matter. Try again. Fail again. Fail better.

Samuel Beckett

Why put money in a fat pig?

Create something that motivates people to save. Design a moneybox to tantalize and excite the saver whenever they insert money. Is it interactive? Help them to be the architect of their own futures and make their dreams happen.

It's a kind of spiritual snobbery that makes people think they can be happy without money.

Albert Camus

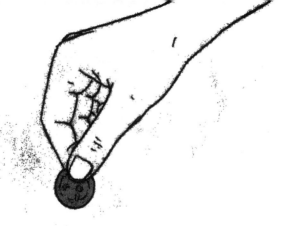

DESIGN A SEDUCTIVE MONEYBOX

Beauty is in the eye of the credit card holder

Your credit card conveys your bank's branding and ethos. Draw what you'd like to see when you use it. The message could be visual or typographical. You're at the till, you're about to buy a gold-plated bath tap, Tunnock's Tea Cake or crocodile-skin umbrella. What do you want to say to yourself? Design the back and front.

Money is a poor man's credit card.

Marshall McLuhan

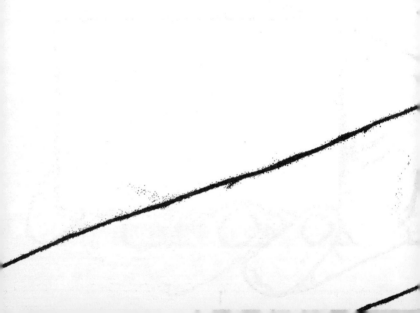

DESIGN YOUR PERSONAL CREDIT CARD

Value is a perception

Transform this one-dollar plastic bucket into a one hundred thousand dollar bucket without spending money. Do something to this bucket that alters the perception of it into something of high status and demand.

The salability of an item can often be improved while the value itself remains unchanged.

Roy H. Williams

MAKE THIS PLASTIC BUCKET VALUABLE

Are you confused?

This chapter is about the challenges of finding your way in a disorienting world. The great feature about our culture is that everything is in a constant state of flux. You need to adapt to the chaotic deluge of the postmodern world to be able to swim in it and not drown. Global information, emails, twenty-four hour news, apps, ads, posters and social media. A 'pic 'n mix' culture. Do you sometimes feel confused? There is no longer an objective 'right' or 'wrong,' it's all a matter of individual opinion. What is good design to one person is bad to another. What is moral in one society is immoral in another. There are no agreed standards of morality so no one has the right to judge another's beliefs. Truth is variable and not absolute so you can make up your own principles.

Cultural relativism is the dominant characteristic of our culture. Our melting pot of cosmopolitanism, multiculturalism and global tourism has mashed layers and layers of different histories and cultures together. You have to make sense of the constant cabaret of paradoxical stories the media toss out for yourself. We swim in a society where absolutes have been abolished, identity has been eroded and everything is subjected to constant revision. We see everything from multiple perspectives and truth shifts according to your viewpoint.

There are no more rigid absolutes to confine us. What if, instead of searching for the 'right way', you search for the 'creative way?' What if you cultivate a sense of joy about the uncertain, constantly look at the world with a fresh pair of eyes and search for the creative possibilities in the chaos? Being open to new ideas enables you to take advantage of opportunities and hack your own path through the jungle.

Life can never be too disorienting.

Guy Debord

A crack dealer's life in the Chicago Projects is dangerous

Standing on street corners makes them visible to customers but susceptible to drive-by shootings from rival gangs. They need to be a difficult target to hit, like the dazzle ships of World War 1. The crisscrossing and intersecting geometric patterns of dazzle didn't conceal the ship like camouflage but made it difficult to judge its distance and movement. Rather than helping anyone find the crack dealer, help him lose himself.

If you can't dazzle them with brilliance, baffle them with bull.

WC Fields

DESIGN A DAZZLE OUTFIT

What does Nowhere look like?

We constantly refer to Nowhere: 'Going Nowhere,' 'It leads Nowhere,' 'Get Nowhere fast,' or 'Miles from Nowhere.' Every country has its own stamps – visualise Nowhere in this set.

Hollywood is like being nowhere and talking to nobody about nothing.

Michelangelo Antonioni

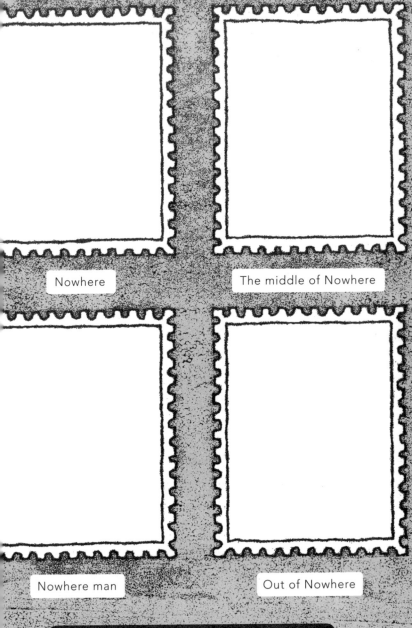

Nowhere

The middle of Nowhere

Nowhere man

Out of Nowhere

DESIGN POSTAGE STAMPS FOR NOWHERE

Do you have an appetite for thought?

Amazingly, some people eat dinner without considering its philosophical, cultural and moral significance. Were the ingredients ethically produced? The farmer fairly paid? Does the meal reflect your beliefs, religion, laws and national identity? Why are particular foods eaten on specific days? Is it a celebratory, ritualistic or symbolic meal? The design on your plate must force the diner to think instead of consuming mindlessly.

To eat is a necessity, but to eat intelligently is an art.

La Rochefoucauld

FORCE FEED THOUGHT

Your client is a ghost

Can you see them? What is their product or service? Do they even exist? To promote and brand a business you have to create a clear, instantly recognizable image and name. You need to communicate its unique abilities via a card. But what are they?

I think I am a better ghost than I am a human being.

Ingmar Bergman

Bacteria constantly mutate and transform

By the time an antidote is found, they've already developed into another form. Bacterial infections are the major threat to human health. As antibiotic resistant superbugs multiply, the fight back takes the form of engineered Phages, viruses that infect and destroy bacteria. Design a virus in this petri dish. Make it even more multi-faceted, fluid and adaptable than bacteria. Attack!

How is it that you keep mutating and can still be the same virus?

Chuck Palahniuk

Can you advertise without advertising?

The Sex Shop sells bondage clothes, magazines, blow-up-dolls, lingerie, sex toys and lubes. Shops use their bags as adverts, and customers promote them as they walk along the street. But a sex shop customer wants to be discreet. Your problem is to design a bag that promotes the shop, subtly.

Sex without love is a meaningless experience, but as far as meaningless experiences go it's pretty damn good.

Woody Allen

DESIGN A BAG FOR THE SEX SHOP

Were you born in the right body?

'His and Hers' towels prevent a couple mixing them up.
You're designing a pair for a gender-fluid couple. Help them
avoid muddling up their towels.

Not a boy or a girl, not any binary, rigid definition of a person.

Leah Raeder, Cam Girl

DESIGN 'HIS AND HERS' TOWELS FOR A GENDER-FLUID COUPLE

Take a deep breath

The idea of free, tasteless water available from any tap being bottled and sold was laughable. But a tsunami of mineral water flooded the globe, creating a billion dollar industry. Your product is air. Convince people it's somehow special and unique. Promote its exclusive qualities in the design.

With a little more tweaking, we could make orange juice in the orange without any packaging or processing.

Homaro Cantou

Coming to a street near you – hip hop architecture

A mashup is a new song assembled from elements of other, pre-existing tracks. Musical snippets are spliced together, new and old, rock and classic, Eastern and Western, to reflect our culture's exposure to myriad different styles. Design a mashup building for this street.

Eclecticism is the degree zero of contemporary general culture: one listens to reggae, watches a western, eats McDonald's food for lunch and local cuisine for dinner, wears Paris perfume in Tokyo and 'retro' clothes in Hong Kong; knowledge is a matter for TV games.

Jean-François Lyotard

DESIGN A MASHUP BUILDING

We buy our way into existence

Our purchases define us. 'I shop therefore I am', declared Barbara Kruger. Commercialization and branding are epidemics. The cure is a movement called Anti Brand, launched to fight back against corporate marketing. They need a logo to summarize their values. Design it on this T-shirt, their first piece of merchandising.

When Nike says, just do it, that's a message of empowerment. Why aren't the rest of us speaking to young people in a voice of inspiration?

Naomi Klein

DESIGN A LOGO FOR ANTI BRAND

Are you lost for words?

Whether you have a way with words or are sometimes beyond words, this chapter helps you to deconstruct language before it deconstructs you. Because ideas and meanings are formed through language, it follows that the structure of language is the key to meaning. We think in words, therefore language shapes our thinking. Language literally creates truth. Meaning comes from the way words are used. Friedrich Nietzsche explained, 'There are no eternal facts, just as there are no absolute truths.' No historian can describe a true event because no one can be truly objective. Everything is dependent on the author's perspective, their particular biases and their culture assumptions. Words can be manipulated to alter the perception of any event.

Text is what language looks like. Typography is the visual manifestation of the spoken word, and a written word's design, the font used, the spacing, the weight and the style, is as much part of its meaning as its content. People rarely think about typography in the same way fish don't think about water. The design of the letters has a psychological effect that can alter the understanding of the message, without anyone realizing. In the film *The Holiday* a character asks a designer to make some type 'Twice as big…but try it in a red. Like a happy red, not a Scorsese red.' Again, the medium is the message.

Philosophy is a battle against the bewitchment
of our intelligence by means of language.

Ludwig Wittgenstein

What do you care about most?

Performance art? Tunnock's Tea Cakes? Carp fishing? Start up a fanzine (an unprofessional magazine produced by a devotee for pleasure) based on your passion, no matter how obscure. Design the front cover and title of the first edition. It must create impact and instantly hook people.

The day I got my first letter from a fan, I felt like I'd been touched by an angel.

Selena Gomez

How did letters evolve?

The earliest words were sketched on the walls of Mesopotamian temples. The alphabet is now fixed at twenty-six letters. It used to be more flexible, with letters regularly coming and going. There was no letter 'U' in Roman times because the letter 'V' represented both the 'V' and 'U' sounds. In ancient England 'Y' represented the sound 'th', as in ye olde shoppe. In the nineteenth century, '&' was an alphabet letter. What new letter do we need? Sketch it next to these oldest ever letters.

The limits of my language are the limits of my mind.
All I know is what I have words for.

Ludwig Wittgenstein

CREATE A NEW LETTER FOR THE ALPHABET

What shape is the letter 'a'?

It can't be defined, yet we recognize it when we see it. There are an
infinite number of possible deviations. We distinguish a letter becaus
of a basic, general shape the variations keep within. Try to make as
many different letter 'a's as possible. Here are three to start you off.

Words are, of course, the most powerful drug used by mankind.

Rudyard Kiplin

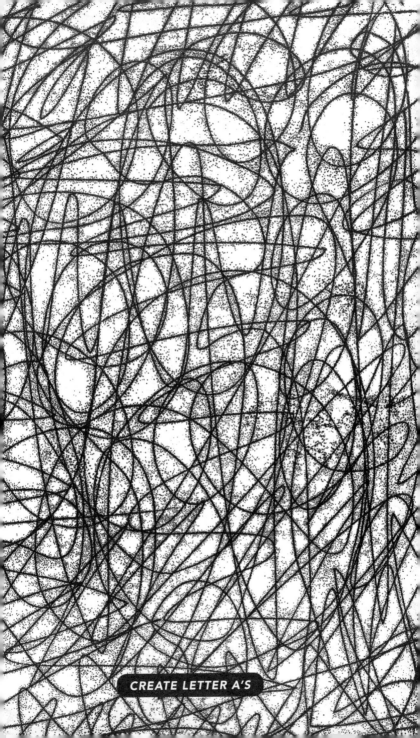

CREATE LETTER A'S

Left on the shelf

A shelf full of intellectual, quirky books can amaze. But to really astound, you need an intellectual, quirky bookshelf. Ron Arad created the innovative and bendable Bookworm Shelf. Made with flexible plastic, it can be bent into any shape. It opened the floodgates to other revolutionary designs. Display your books with inventiveness.

A man's bookcase will tell you everything you'll ever need to know about him.

Walter Mosley

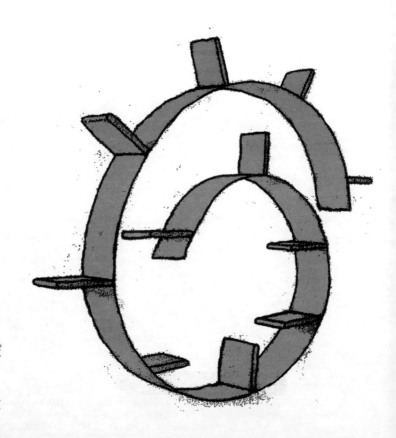

DESIGN A BOOKSHELF

What does chaos look like typographically?

CDs of various audio sounds are available, from those of nature (waves breaking on the shore, trees rustling, rain falling) to those of the city (cars honking, engines revving, ambulances blaring). Your CD contains the sound of chaos. According to Chaos Theory, chaos and order are inextricably linked. One can't exist without the other. Use only lettering to design your cover.

Art, in itself, is an attempt to bring order out of chaos.

Stephen Sondheim

DESIGN A CD COVER FOR THE SOUND OF CHAOS

Don't read this

The ability to read and write enables us to fulfill our potential and grasp opportunities. When adults prosper, their families, communities and employers also benefit. Persuade the illiterate it's worth going back to class. But note, the people your poster is targeting can't read.

People don't realize how a man's whole life can be changed by one book.

Malcolm X

What's your story?

What is special about you? Don't use illustration, limit yourself to typography. Restrict yourself to the generic title 'my autobiography' and use the design of the lettering to convey the meaning. And remember, we judge a book by its cover.

Writing Charles Dickens' biography was like writing five biographies.

Claire Tomalin

DESIGN THE FRONT COVER OF YOUR AUTOBIOGRAPHY

You're doomed to fail

Embossed letters! Drop shadows! Comic Sans! Overuse of explanation marks! Typography hell. Typographers are fussy and judgemental about the details of type. They are painstaking about kerning (the space between letters), leading (the space between lines) and tracking (the space between words). Designing type for a typographer is like cutting a hairdresser's hair. They're hypercritical experts and demand perfection, with good reason. The masthead (the design of the magazine's name) doubles as the logo and stays the same for each edition – good luck!

I do not think of type as something that should be readable. It should be beautiful.

Ed Benguiat

Are you hard to please?

A seal is a device for making an impression in wax to authenticate a legal document or envelope. It has more gravitas than a Facebook like. Every pope has their own seal; when they die it's destroyed and a new one for the next pope is created. Create a seal of approval to stamp on something you think is great.

Eventually you just have to realize that you're living for an audience of one. I'm not here for anyone else's approval.

Pamela Anderson

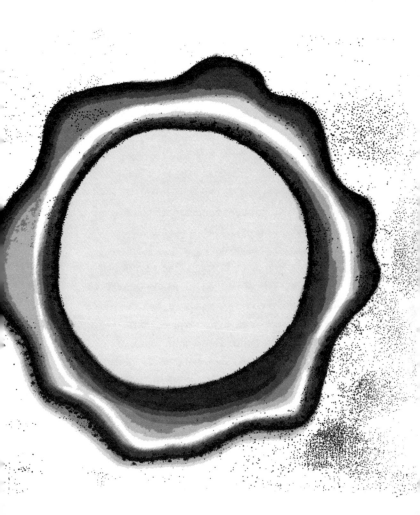

Does a dog's bark sound the same everywhere?

Onomatopoeia is a word that imitates the sound it describes. The 'Bow Wow' theory of linguistics proposes that language emerged from copying animal cries, grunts and snorts.

In Brazil it's spelt au au, in Albania lehje lehje, in China wang wang and in the English-speaking world, woof woof. Arabic: hu hu, Belarusian: hav hav, Bengali: bunana bunana, Bosnian: bau bau, Bulgarian: vutuk vutuk, Croatian: vau vau, Czech: haf haf, Dutch: woef woef, Estonian: auh auh, Finish: hau hau, French: ouah ouah, Greek: yfadi yfadi, Hebrew: beeeyoo beeeyoo, German: wau wau, Hungarian: vau vau, Indonesian: guk guk, Korean: ssi ssi, Japanese: wan wan, Korean: meong meong, Latvian: audi audi, Lithuanian: au au, Maori: aho aho, Mongolian: khav khav, Norwegian: voff voff, Polish: hau hau, Polish: watek watek, Portugese: trama trama, Punjabi: fafudi fafudi, Romanian: batatura batatura, Russian: gav gav, Samoan: vav vav, Serbian: voof voof, Slovak: haf haf, Slovenian: ujeti ujeti, Somali: gudubsan gudubsan, Spanish: guau guau, Swedish: voff voff, Tamil: utu utu, Thai: hong hong, Yiddish: vuf vuf, Zulu: evundlile evundlile.

We are all mediators, translators.

Jacques Derrida

INVENT A WORD TO DESCRIBE HOW YOU
THINK A DOG'S BARK REALLY SOUNDS

Epilogue

At this point, you're probably thinking you've reached the end of the book. Wrong. This is the beginning. Now your task is to continue your 'idea thinking' in the street, workplace and home, to become a mint of ideas inspired by the objects and services surrounding you.

This book proposes *ideas are currency*. If you have an idea that literally makes you money, that's great. But this book is really about how ideas enrich you and the world you live in. They have worth beyond monetary value. Ideas are a medium of exchange circulating throughout the culture and opening up opportunities. They create both small incremental progress but also revolutionary advances transforming every field, law, education, banking, biotech, engineering, healthcare, InfoTech, the list goes on... The more ideas there are in the world, the better it becomes. The more ideas occur in medicine, the healthier we become, the more ideas in aeronautical engineering, the safer our aircraft and in the energy sector, the more renewable sources. That's why the book touches on technology, values, the future and many other important themes of culture.

The purpose of these exercises was to help you flex and develop your idea generating muscles. But my intention in this and my other books is to help you develop into a fluid thinker, thriving on instability because it opens up opportunities. Skills have a sell-by date but an ideas person can adapt to future developments. Although computers increasingly take over, a nomadic, entrepreneurial mind surpasses them in fields requiring creativity, emotional intelligence or entrepreneurship.

To prepare yourself for the world of the future you need to invest in yourself. I hope this book has in some small way helped you with that process.

Acknowledgements

I'd like to thank my daughter, Scarlet Judkins for designing all the layouts for the rough draft, suggesting ideas and helping to design the composition of the pages. Zelda Malan for her honest and therefore invaluable criticism of the exercises and for suggesting improvements to the layouts, illustrations and alternative exercises. A remarkable and original creative thinker, she promotes 'idea thinking' at Kingston University and has been a huge influence on the book. Thanks to Louis Judkins for being the model for many of the illustrations and for his opinions on the projects.

Thanks to Drummond, my editor at Sceptre for commissioning the book and for all his support, enthusiasm, suggestions and ideas. Craig Burgess's art direction really polished up the book and helped create the look and feel I was searching for. I'm grateful to the team at Sceptre for creating the cover.

Thanks to my agent Jonathan Conway for all his support and belief in this book. I'm grateful to Jonathan for extracting the title, *Ideas Are Your Only Currency*, from the text in my first draft of the book.

Thanks to my colleagues and students at the universities where I work for their generosity in suggesting occasional lines and ideas – too numerous to mention them all here but The School of Life, Central Saint Martins, University College London, City Lit and The London College of Fashion deserve a special thanks.

The line, 'C-beams glittering in the dark near the Tannhäuser Gate', is quoted from the film *Blade Runner*. 'You gotta say yes to another excess' is a quote from Yello.

All illustrations by Rod Judkins

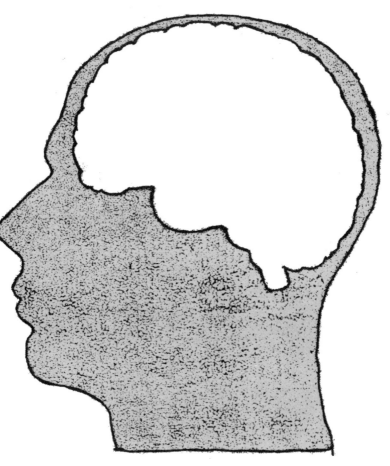

DRAW THE CONTENTS OF
YOUR MIND NOW.

**Ideas are your only currency –
NOW IT'S TIME TO INVEST.**

Z983854